Venus
in pink marble

Venus
in pink marble

Gaynor Kane

First published 2020 by The Hedgehog Poetry Press

Published in the UK by
The Hedgehog Poetry Press
Coppack House, 5
Churchill Avenue
Clevedon
BS21 6QW

www.hedgehogpress.co.uk

ISBN: 978-1-913499-31-0

Copyright © Gaynor Kane 2020
Cover design © 2789 Graphic Design, Newcastle, County Down, N. Ireland
Illustrations © Gaynor Kane

The right of Gaynor Kane to be identified as the author of this work has been asserted in accordance with the Copyright, Designs and Patents Act 1988.

All rights reserved. No part of this publication may be reproduced, stored in or introduced into a retrieval system, or transmitted in any form, or by any means (electronic, mechanical, photocopying, recording or otherwise) without prior written permissions of the publisher. Any person who does any unauthorised act in relation to this publication may be liable for criminal prosecution and civil claims for damages,

9 8 7 6 5 4 3 2 1

A CIP Catalogue record for this book is available from the British Library.

For Michael and Tara

with love

Paper Boats

for Mark Davidson

They
were fragile,
translucent, folded
edges crisp and straight.
His hulls held

her
poems;
words of love,
loss, and grief, their weight
made immense by the tremble of his hand.

Crouched at water's edge,
sand shifting beneath his feet,
he fed them to the sea,
placed on the apex of waves, to float out fast.

He looked across the grey expanse
to where she lay sleeping deep,
dreaming of patterned pages,
embossed serpents' tongues.

Off they tugged on mourning moon-tide;
he wished them safe passage
but did not see
his red ink bleeding
and rice paper dissolving
before they reached the skyline.

Contents

Section 1: The Lock

Paper Boats 7

The Lock 12

Echoes 14

Goliath Tree, Victoria Park 15

Wolf tree 16

The Port of the Bog 17

Dead Short on the System, Belfast, 1923. 18

Annadale, 22nd April 1914 19

Domestic Help 1916 20

Christmas Morning, Carrowdore, 1870 21

From Benin to Belfast 22

Wully Yeaman, at the Punch Ball, Carrowdore 24

Only Footprints 25

Belfast Moon, January 2017 26

It's an economic issue 27

Duck, duck, goose 28

Election Day, 12th December 2019 29

Home 30

Section 2: Letter to Me

Letter to Me 35

Recipe For the Scent of You 36

Barometer 37

Gran's Biscuit Tin 38

The first time I saw him cry 40

That's Debatable 41

Trussed 42

Birthmark 43

Foot Reading 44

Faith 46

Coupes 47

Bridging 48

Polyester 49

Fire-lighting 50

The Wishbone 51

Job No. 1621 52

Friday Thirteenth 53

Window Weather 54

Cross Roads 55

Spring Bank Holiday 56

Tollymore 57

Dreamchild 58

Princess of Eiderdown 59

Spiderman 60

Little Novice 61

Biologist 62

Section 3: A Life Drawn

A Life Drawn 67

American Gothic 68

A Lifetime Later 69

Herd 70

I Am Not Prepared 71

Reportage 72

Lemniscate 74

Little Magician 75

Handwritten 76

Demolition 77

The Starry Night 78

The World's Most Dangerous Harpist 79

The Vampire of Lazzaretto Vecchio 80

At Castle Ward 81

Scrabo Cheirotherium Fossil 82

The Day the Painting Came Alive 83

Still life with hedgehog 84

Notes and Glossary 87

Section 1

The Lock

The Lock

I can't resist the challenge
        of working out your code.
Listen to the click, click, click
        of teeth nipping past the pin.
Listen for the tock of the clock,
        as the dials rotate.
Listen for ticks of numbers falling
        in place and your combo clunk.

You meet my nose with coldness
        and the scent of blood,
new-borns, and his collection
        of copper coins. Mother's gold
charm bracelet with clover, wishing well,
        clog and key. Or her grandfather's
old toolbox, a cacophony of giants:
        chisels, claw-hammer, hacksaw, caulk.

Your colour has me thinking
        of boulders along the edge
of Belfast Lough, where O'Neill's red
        hand alighted after being cleaved
and hurled from sea to land.
        Or mountains of fossilised rocks,
stacked at the docks. Coal carted,
        then scooped in spade loads into sacks.

You are tugboat shaped,
        my thoughts go large to Arrol gantries
and liners nesting within skeletal stocks,
        until fully formed. Rivets struck
like rhythmic heartbeats. Chocks lodged
        in place, to stop them slipping out to sea,
until waters broke and ships
        were birthed by tugboat midwives.

Everything was monochrome, chalk, smoke,
        firebrick, slack. Dunchers, dungarees,
grubby hands and faces at clocking-off,
        men's boots still gleaming with pride.
Pride passed down paternally,
        reflecting on shiny surfaces,
until the yard was boat-less, barren,
        and the gates all locked.

Echoes

Industrial bones in the landscape; outlines,
corridors, old tracks, where nature
reclaims shadows and buddleias bloom.
Reverb in shape and form of streets
waste-ground, skeletal structures, pulleys,
winches, big metal rings for hanging things.

Ghost signs and negatives etched
on buildings, pointers to the past,
in kerbs and cobbles, ornate ironwork.
Backyards with outhouses, coal stores,
a rusty tin bath hung from a nail.

Stagnant water's slow-flow framework
where once it was dynamic, the lifeblood
of linen weavers, rope makers, shipbuilders;
now ancient streams and forgotten dreams.

Goliath Tree, Victoria Park

When the storm, with the Irish boy's name, came
my leaves fell early, were swept aside to dry and curl,
like arthritic hands of a redundant shipyard worker.

In them you might see rusty beakers, handmade paper,
black-pepper pods, burnt Belfast brick,
freshly ploughed fields, the speckled plumage of a thrush,
a wooden jetty over gently flowing water.

They are paperweight – lighter than a pebble,
heavier than a feather – with the strength
of a mahogany boat, on water they will float.

Lift my leaf, hold it cradled in your hands,
let curled fingers cup your cheek.
You might smell where fresh water meets sea-tide.
The scent of the park, the Oval, the Yard
and our industrial ghosts.

Wolf tree

Last night, under a super blue blood moon,
I heard him howl, crowned by an eerie halo.
Firmly fixed for centuries, singing tunes
to faeries, dancing, as the wind whispers low.

Bent from hangings of witch and shrew;
innocent or guilty, local folk were watchers.
Gnarled limbs, torture cubs with corkscrew
claws. Crows caw at the sight of his canker.

Branded with W, wolf, witness, wise-one
but aloof; refusing to speak through his roots
of things seen in histories long gone.
Days lengthen, he grows bright green shoots.

The Port of the Bog

Its purpose is woven
into the landscape.

East Strand,
a beach of shells:
mussels, clams.
Cast overboard,
washed up; stranded.
Above the high tide line,
are lobster pot pyramids.

Stone walls pincushion
bleached-wood net needles;
colourful markers, buoys
and floats, decorate gardens.
Lawns are quilted by drying nets.
The harbour seal, circles,
disturbs oily rainbows.

Ebb and flow histories,
the rise and fall
of quotas,
trawlers trailed to bog-land.
Burnt.

Those who remember
and those who don't.

Dead Short on the System, Belfast, 1923.

Every trolleybus and tram frozen,
stopped dead on the first evening
of a new year – dark, damp
and sticky like a new-born.

Across the city, cars are static
blocking streets and junctions
like snakes and ladders.
Those tram-trapped, fear
the curfew more than the rain.

Moments before the blackout
a rat wandered aimlessly
into a high-voltage power-station,
to lazily chew through copper cables.

It was found the following day,
fused to circuit, curled teeth
still clamped around the wires, pink ears,
black currant eyes, rigor-straight legs,
while outside, trams trundled.

Annadale, 22nd April 1914

She stands silhouetted, on the towpath,
against a moonlit Lagan lapping.
I know I share intent
with this unknown suffragette.

We show each other simple arms:
paraffin, matches, rags; walk in silence
towards our target, its large chimney stacks
visible above treelined horizon.

Moonshine turns the roof's
Belfast-blue slates, silvery.
Across the river two hares, upright,
almost nose-to-nose, sizing
each other up, wondering who'd thump first.

We place our leaflets in the roots
of apple trees, low branches of soft fruits;
line the tennis courts with row
upon row of *Votes for Women*.

Hitch our skirts and climb the walls
like acrobats. She soap-smears
the windowpane. I lift a broken brick
and smash the glass to smithereens.

Scoot down the stairs, stuff scented rags
into the pantry, the hot-press; strike matches,
drop them, watch flames furrow quarry tiles,
flickering tongues of our voice.

In the ballroom, a golden dawn
has set the room aglow. The cobwebbed
chandeliers reflect light across
the mirrors and gilded ornaments.

We waltz, still strangers. After one
revolution, I look into the black
well of her eyes, curtsy, leave.
Never to see her again.

Domestic Help 1916

Come on! Come on! Cumann na mBan
Throw poetry, prose, plays and pistols
into a pot and let the women serve
a revolutionary banquet. Be radical
with hotel larders and factory biscuits,
to create rations for the regiments. Train her
in rifles, rounds and revival. Teach her
to be alert, brave and cunning.
Come on! Come on! Cumann na mBan

Sacrifice your safety, sideboard
and sofas, to barricade the streets.
Dance dangerously with the men
from last week's céilí, then take
orders, tapping keys to the tune
of the rebels' refrain, hear the music
of the Mauser's bodhrán beat.
Come on! Come on! Cumann na mBan

Spread your wings and fly across the
scarlet skyline, unruffled by scorching
cinder confetti. Or scurry through streets
and alleys, under the disguise of
your sex, moving arms and ammo unseen.
Weave underground networks, in a city
divided by more than the Liffey.
Come on! Come on! Cumann na mBan

Bandage the bullet wounds and dress
the damage done by colonial oppression;
these scars will mark you forever.
Raise the blood-stained sheet, and mourn
the child that, for six days,
fought for life . Don't wear black;
say *I do* under the shadow of death,
against the executioner's ticking clock.

Christmas Morning, Carrowdore, 1870

On the horizon of Carney Brae, hats dawn;
Bowlers, Tam O'Shanters, Stovepipes,
sprouting from turf like seed husks on shoots.

Blown in, on a north-easterly from lowlands, over water,
to The Low Country. Sons of the sod, cotters and plewmen,
camouflaged by breeks and frock coats of sage and heather tweed.

Fog, patches a landscape eiderdown.
The village iced, pure and clean. Above, Orion
is fading; as the tide tugs the sun from slumber.

Christ Church is swallowed, only its steeple
rises above mist. They had watched it grow,
from the ground, stone by Scrabo stone.

Rifles ready to find a festive feast, they scan
the Squire's land in silence; breath billowing
like smoke breathing dragons, angered at rack rents.

Index finger touches nose, reaches into the distance,
Eye contact relays round like silent toppling dominoes.
Dogs point, noses and tails, akin to compass needles.

A goose, busy plucking moss, invisible no longer, as the sun
has thawed her tummock. Bowler hat fires the shot, his shoulder
takes pain first. Smoke burns the air; sulphur suffocates.

The goose lies up-field, neck contorted, her beak ajar,
scarlet feathers flying; falling. In a circle of congratulation,
they pat each other *Merry Christmas*.

From Benin to Belfast

Benin boy whittles under shade
of oil palms and cocoa plants. Plagued
by flies, wishing for a spare hand or tail
to swish, like the bony cattle.
He's told it is a great honour
to prepare ivory for the mask
that will adorn Oba's hip.
Elephant blood stains ground red.

Guild man, seventeen now,
commissioned to make two new masks.
Portuguese trade has built the Oba
towers of gold, his palace must
be decorated in precious metal.
The man's hands are chafed,
burnt from smoke smelting
bronze, his eyes strained red.

Ten years later, the same Edo man
is hung from a tree on the end
of an Imperial rope. Crafters guild all suffer
the same fate, red sap flowing down trunks,
blood puddles. Queen Mother's ivory
mask and Benin bronzes stowed away
on Admiral Rawson's ship. Oba's palace
razed; glowing ash is molten red.

***

A locally crafted shoe, in a cobwebbed
corner of the Ulster museum, now stands
looking down on the mask. I think
of the adopted baby you paraded
up and down the Crumlin Road in a Silver Cross,
as the Civil Rights movement,
and the country's troubles grew,
but you were unaware of them.

You longed to nurture that baby,
with dark tight curls the colour of leather
your father cobbled into boots.
Splintered on finding baby's house
broken; busted windows, burnt doorframe,
her little red shoe on the threshold.
At Sunday Mass the whole parish
staring through their ivory masks.

Wully Yeaman, at the Punch Ball, Carrowdore

You think how pretty she is; curls
stacked like hay on top of her crown,
how clever she is to have drawn-on
dance pumps, with shoe polish.

You watch her from across the barn,
her boots placed preciously under bench,
she points her toes, draws slow circles,
like cartwheels, in the sawdust.

Harry takes her to dance, no question
of acceptance - she does as bid.
They hold the crowd's gaze, whirling
together, like a spinning top.

You think how stupid he is taking Agnes
to dance. You must have a talk outside.
Everyone in the village knows
she's your sweetheart; it's a matter of honour.

You watch from the fringes, frowning,
fists clenched before stepping out. The bull is charging
the plough, you catch Harry's eye,
signal with a nod, a thumb over the shoulder.

Temper's aisy riz, you cross the back field,
take off your coat, roll up both sleeves.
Like looking at glass, he mirrors your actions.
One punch and the Punch Ball is over for another year.

Only Footprints

"nobody can take those footsteps I made
on the surface of the moon away from me"
Eugene Cernan

Walking the beach at Castlerock
angled against strong wind. Everything slant –
grasses, birds, spray from white horses,
the hail when it comes.

Miles ahead and miles behind stretches
of fine cappuccino-coloured sand. The churning
sea has left a creamy foam. I lift one perfect
side of razor shell to bring home.

What will you do with it when you go?
Leave it behind; like a footprint, or blade
in my heart? The signs say there have been
no children here today.

Small patterns from kittiwakes, herring
gulls, gannets and guillemots. Dogs
and adults have left prints too.
Hail has blurred the horizon.

Returning to the car I notice
a path through the dunes; a total
tapestry of treads and wonder
if it's a genetic imprint

to leave our mark? In the grasses
there are coffee cups,
water bottles, fishing wire,
torn rags, rope and plastic bags.

I think of Gene tramping the lunar
landscape, leaving stamps on astral
ash. Man's last special steps
on the surface of the moon.

Belfast Moon, January 2017

Venus and Mars
are fighting
for your attention.
Trying to dazzle you
with mythological muscle.
Spheres spinning in alignment.
Longing to caress
the silvery curve
of your crescent.

From my Crescent
they look perfectly positioned.
Like threaded ocean pearls
on pure black satin
or golden embers
on a boiler floor.

It's stifling hot
in Stormont. They had
the windows open
all over Christmas.
Searching for
a sign, a star,
or wise men in the East.
No saviour found, just dark
powers colliding;
integrity
compromised.

It's an economic issue

Yesterday, western eyes focused
on America's hurricane fear.
But *climate change doesn't exist.*

Yesterday, in Mongolia, a toddler
lay in an intensive care ward
on a clean sheet of red and blue
strawberries. Hooked up to machines
monitoring her blackened pneumonia lungs.
Her forehead is smudged with black ash
- to ward off evil spirits, thinks her Mum
but it's coal pollution that's malevolent.

Yesterday's Western child cried #Instatears
for the National Geographic image of a crane
bagged in a transparent shroud,
beak poking through but breathless.
Clingfilmed wings. Stranded and suffocating;
a living ghost.

Yesterday, yellow gantries rumbled
on rusty shipyard tracks in Belfast.
Monumental metal trestles, flat plateau
of Cavehill a giant sized table-top.
Meccanno oil rig platforms bolted together
and round metal turbine towers for wind power.
The receivers moved in.
Freezing workers camped outside in protest.

Duck, duck, goose

The first year they arrived, people made jokes about there being just enough time to fatten them up for Christmas dinner. Wee wimmun, in rollered headscarves, slippers, slacks and anoraks, came out daily with leftovers and the prized heel of the plain loaf (the thick one, not the skittery one). Dogs, that once roamed the estate freely, now chained-up – howling, hungry mouths foaming.

Liberal Icelandic Greylags flew across thousands of miles of sea, to land in the Lower Shankill on The Green and the signs (that no one seemed to see) said *No Games*. Greylags, with greyscale peppered plumage, paraded around the square. But things are black-and-white here, except murals, red hands and camouflage commandos.

Big men, with puffed-out chests, strutted about warning that no necks were to be wrung, not even a single feather ruffled. These birds had their heads nestled under loyalist paramilitaries' wings. In Spring, they took to the skies in skeins of V for victory. Now returning annually, just before Remembrance Day wreaths are laid.

Election Day, 12th December 2019

They hung them out
on inner-city church railings,
like multi-coloured tree decorations.
On telegraph poles
large beaming faces,
of the would-be-elected,
look down from on high.

The starving and shivering
flock, like pigeons after crumbs,
to the parkas and padded jackets,
North Face, Regatta, Superdry,
the jumpers with snowflakes and red noses.
He asks if there's one that would fit.
Just one, he doesn't want to be greedy.

As dark puddles twinkle with reflected lights
from the Christmas Market helter-skelter
he takes to the shop door for shelter.
Across town, in a sports hall, black boxes
are opened. A hail of white on tables, slush piles
and warm hands scooping handfuls of ballot-paper-snow.
Counting crosses.

Home

Under the shadow of the world's largest cranes, the girl in the designer tracksuit weaves around the Saturday shoppers, as they saunter through the city streets arms evenly laden with plastic carrier bags. She is even quicker past the beggar, slouched against empty shop hoardings in Castle Arcade. Until - she sees the dog - stops - fetches out a rawhide bone. Without making eye contact she realises the homeless girl only has a cardboard box windbreaker for shelter, a crocheted baby blanket draped over spider thin limbs. Her exposed skin is snail-grey.

guilt makes her scoop change
covered in pocket fluff, coppers
jangle in begging bowl

***

I'm transfixed by the Arachnid's ingenuity, she is hydraulic jack, trolley, removal van, crane. Spinning her gossamer strands, up and down between branch and new abode. Relentlessly. With each revolution her house is a sliver higher into the safety of leaf cover. She is so small, a seed husk with legs. Her rope is fragile fine. But having sensed there is a storm coming, she has a plan for shelter and I can see her determination. I make lunch, put a wash on, brush up leaf drifts from corners and kerbs and when I return to check on her, she is almost home.

snail long departed,
pearlescent with rain, vacant shell
now a sanctuary

***

I think of you, all those years ago. After the Ulster Workers' Council strike in the 1970s, when I made toast in front of the open fire because we'd no electric or gas. The UDA put Betty into the empty house down our street (rumour had it she never paid a day's rent in her life). By the time the strike was over the firm you worked for had gone bust because they'd lost so many contracts. You exhausted your web of contacts; the telegraph job section was thin. But the mortgage needed paid and Mummy couldn't clean enough houses to cover it. You went to Liverpool for work.

docked where the slave ships
sailed from. Scoured the streets for digs
no blacks, no dogs, no Irish

Section 2

Letter to Me

Letter to Me

Do not take advice from me.
You have foresight and everything
happens for a reason.

Aren't you stronger for knowing
how close you came to replicating
the mistake your mother made,

instead you had the strength to grab
your bag and run to the roundabout,
in bare feet and nightie, never looking back?

Isn't your leg more interesting with the little
dot-dot-dot – dash – dot-dot-dot faded stitch scar,
cut by a falling vase, as the phone cord

tried to strangle it, when the Dubliner
that you'd spent a handful of hours, face
to face with, was proposing marriage?

Didn't you find the fear of being
out of your depth was irrelevant, when you
were dragged through the deep blue and survived?

How light you felt moments before that,
suspended hundreds of metres above the coast
of Zakynthos, harnessed to your best friend?

Don't change your wedding plans,
or doublecheck
that everything is packed.

Recipe For the Scent of You

i.m Winnie McCutcheon

Add two parts Sunlight soap
and one of Brasso or Vim
(depending on the day)
to Yardley's *Lily of the Valley*.
Beat with vigour, wearing a floral pinafore
fold in chocolate and desiccated coconut.
Cut into squares – your signature traybake.
Top with a dusting of pressed powder
and Max Factor cherry-red lipstick.

Barometer

Every visit, I tapped it religiously
as if godly power
or magnetism
were at work.
I couldn't pass through
the hallway without studying

its face. Like yours,
it measured the pressure,
forecast the atmosphere;
the weatherglass predicted
dry or rain,
fair or stormy.
A gentle pat would see the needle
swing from one to the other.

Just as a hug
would thaw you,
crow's-feet and laughter lines
breaking your ice.

Gran's Biscuit Tin

I borrowed it from a cousin
hoping to add colourful leaves
to a bare tree. On the base,
Inglis' Bakery claims creation;
a family firm bred locally.

Perhaps the crumbs
of biscuits eaten long ago,
dusted the lips, on faces
in pictures now nestled
in its tarnished silver lining.

Lid trimmed at the edges
with dry, cracked, tape
curling like Autumn
leaves, in sepia,
like the photos within,

and topped with a scene,
not a chocolate-box cottage,
but a fishing village,
reminiscent of Clovelly,
Lynmouth or Hope Cove.

I look at the postcards
inside and try to find
a connection, discovering
one from my father,
as young man, on honeymoon.

They travelled to Dun Laoghaire,
not Devon, and from their room
in the Carney Arms
they watched snow
fall like confetti,

blurring with white sails
and sea spray in the bay.
I trace the signature,
follow the fancy scroll
of his $\mathcal{T}$ and $\mathcal{V}$.

From my desk, the tin watches
seasons pass like old friends.
Now and then, I leaf
through the photos hoping
to put names to faces,

examining expressions,
noses and chins, for family
similarities, then peruse
the back, still longing
for a lightly leaded name.

The first time I saw him cry

We were eating fish and homemade chips
deep-fried in the best butcher's lard,
when Johnny from up the street knocked;
said there was a phone call my father had to take.

Before parading up the hill, round the dogleg
bend, he put his boots back on
lingering to tie the laces. He'd taught
me how, with black liquorice strings.

Pritchard's hallway, a half-heard conversation:
How did it happen? Where is he now?
Tell my Mother I'll be down on the first bus.
Thank you for letting me know.

Holding his hand, we retraced our steps,
looked at the setting sun falling into the docks.
Your Grandda's dead; then he carried on,
thinking that was enough said.

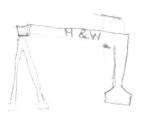

That's Debatable

Two words,
often uttered
in our house
growing up.

Piercing the points
of the sunburst clock,

hanging from
the wire guitar,
like an unfinished
chord, music-less

and silently soaking
into brown & amber wallpaper;

no discussion from either.

Trussed

I read a poem about battle scars, thought how lucky
I am, to have parchment skin, an unmarked body.

A baby, reluctant, sucked out, bald head blistered
like toad skin; leaving the womb half-hearted.

Misshapen, club-footed, forced to wear a splint
moulding pliable bones from bent to straight.

Being restrained was my toddler bedtime
routine, bound in boots, hide straps, brass buckles;

my mother transformed to woodworker,
as if steam-bending a strip of tear-soaked birch.

Sun-bleached walls protected me in daylight,
sitting on drab slabs behind steel spindles;

I was an x-ray, grey, looking out at a rainbow
watching others play, imagining a friend.

***

I grew into my own skin, cast off confinement
shackled no longer I became less wooden;

My scars weren't physical,
they were invisible;

a lover couldn't tell the difference, but I know
that it was my right that was remoulded

and although almost straight, it is dumpier,
branded at the ankle with a paradoxical beauty spot.

Birthmark

How did a strand
of your genes break
off to become part of me?

The pull cord,
a celebratory party
popper, multi-coloured
paper spirals
defying gravity.

And both of us
with a single freckle
on our little toe.

Foot Reading

this is not a kindness
a duty, or a religious metaphor
it is inherent

I fill two basins, rising steam dampens my face, add a few squirts of green, stray bubbles pop against the kitchen window. I ask you to dip a toe, you nod approval, lift the lead weight of your feet, they drop like lumps of land breaking free of the cliffs and falling into sea, sink beneath the surface. Your face relaxes.

blackbirds drop from tree
searching for breakfast leftovers
find nothing but bugs

Every Sunday night (whether I needed it or not, we laugh) you ran my bath, poured in Matey for bubble mohawks, tossed in multi-coloured Tupperware. After being swaddled in cotton, I'd run downstairs and sit on your knee, in the fireside chair, while you dried my hair and between each individual toe, tickled my feet. Compared the single freckle we both have on our right little piggy.

sky turns from orange to red
pink and purple as dusk descends
swifts swoop in circles

Now, your toes sufficiently wrinkled, callouses waxy white, I ease each foot out, wrap them in the towel. Deformed feet, big toes bunioned, corns on phalanges; the result of too many dances in stiletto heeled winkle-pickers. The scissors can cut anything, according to your QVC god, and I have tested this by gliding through a tin of ham.

baby mice, transparent
pink wrinkles, jump from nest
into jack russell's teeth

In turn, I take these to both parents' feet. You have shared fifty-three years and your fungal infections, with each other. Twenty toenails in shades of banana mousse, cream cake and custard, ribbed like palm trees or the shells on the beach.

found in pocket
one heart-shaped stone, polished
smooth by your thumb

I remember going to the Mournes each Easter Monday, to skim for smicks in the Shimna, then later after a picnic of egg and onion sandwiches, tea and biscuits, I would paddle in the Irish Sea, look for razor shells, driftwood, mermaids' purses. Sitting in the boot of the Austin Allegro while you would dry my feet. Carefully pulling the towel between my toes to remove every grain of sand.

Faith

Pigtails, frilly socks, white streaks ran
about collecting buttercups, dandelions,
variegated leaves, butterflies, beetles,
slugs and snails for her 'peep show'
under a large piece of glass. Leaf curtains
kept the surprise safe, while her twin
played with whip and peerie.

Sister spooked cat, one shrieked,
the other screeched; ruby-rose petals
pirouetted to their death.
Sharp claws climbed her
like a scratching post, carved
her cream skin until a red sea
ran down her arms and legs.

Mother plonked her onto the bench,
smeared tears, sterilised shredded
skin, bandaged each limb,
blotted Sunday best. No time
for consolation, only sinners are late
for church. Goose-stepped to St. Brendan's
with stained legs, dress, face.

Kneeling painfully, palms pressed tight,
eyes soldered, she prayed
for forgiveness, prayed for Mother,
prayed for the poor cat,
she imagined cowering in a corner
contemplating how a morning stroll
could go so wrong.

Opening her eyes, clouds part
allowing the sun to filter through stained-glass
windows baptising her in a rainbow
of light, a kaleidoscope of warmth and love,
she takes her mother's hand, silence falls;
from outside she hears a cat meowing
and knows He has heard and answered.

Coupes

for Mum

A stag's head looks down
through soulless sockets,
focuses on fuchsia,
mother-of-pearl sequins;
a gown self-spun
from fifty yards of net.
Black gloves, holding
a single daffodil
at the Floral Hall.

In champagne coupes
baby bubbles bounce;
reflecting light like a mirror ball.
A hand reaches over,
pulls a puff of pink
across the dancefloor;
they spin
laughing and talking
until birds sing.

Bridging

It falls off the tongue
as easy as a river
rolling over rocks.
I can sense
the roll of his eyes
the pinch of wrinkles
the slow shake
of my Hubby's head in despair.

It's six, of, one, and
half a dozen
of the other
he will say, in the way
you talk to tourists
but the warmth
in his words
could cut clouds.

If I was a gambling man
like my father, I would bet
that he taught me
the proverb. In the same way
he showed me how
to spot birds. Thrush,
wren, *mummy*
and *daddy* blackbirds.

Imparting that, starlings
murmuring at dusk,
darkening clouds, whirring
on airwaves and swooping
under the Albert,
like cotton gliding through
the eye of a needle,
was them *getting ready for bed*.

Polyester

Slippered feet on the stone hearth,
feeling the glow. Across our street,
the sky rested on rooftops, heavy,
full of a solstice harvest, hanging.

I was drowning in heat, like a Christmas
pudding drenched in brandy. Then I heard
a sizzle, a crunch, felt fire
licking my hair, hugging my back.

Before I was engulfed by fear
and flames, she threw me on the floor,
rolled me in the mat,
brandy-snapped and smoke-smothered.

Christmas morning, the clouds were bright and empty.
Among the presents was a dressing gown
as white as snow, folded neatly, ribbon-bowed, and labelled
one hundred percent brushed cotton.

Fire-lighting

was art. Like origami; folded,
pressed, turned, folded, pressed, turned
and repeated until fingertips blackened.
The newspaper resembled an accordion
and we sang with pretend accompaniment,
pumping the bellows to the beat. The *Belfast
Telegraph* transformed to squeezeboxes.

It was a skill, like dry-stone walling.
We laid a bed of sticks, then arranged layers
of paper firelighters, more sticks, the occasional
Sunny Jim topped with shiny black nuggets.
Not built too high, to prevent more crop-circles
from appearing on the fireside mat. We carried
cooling ashes, at arm's length, to the bin.

It was dangerous, like lion taming.
You flicked the match against the firebrick,
poked it between the bars to light the paper
before the flame scorched your skin.
We watched as flames seared sticks, charring them,
sparking red as the last sheet of paper
was held at the corners, taut, for the draw.

The Wishbone

Sunday evening saw the chicken picked clean
of all cream flesh. The wishbone
set aside and carcass boiled for stock.

Every morning, as sacred as Stonehenge, the rising
sun perfectly aligned through the furcula's arch,
propped against the pane. Drying it took days.

You wish now that you'd known your ancestors
made theirs with just a stroke. You had to wait
for bone to be brittle. To break.

Siblings absent, you chose Mother each Saturday,
the weaker one, until Father's hands distorted
and you, in your twenties, were still wishing.

Little pinkie perfectly poised, wrapped around
the centre, not the tip (that was a flawed strategy).
You held tight. She pulled. Snap!

You always got to make the wish; eyes clammed
tight to send it into flight. And you can't remember
what you hoped for – or if it ever came true.

Job No. 1621

for Dad

Once, a carpenter on the Canberra,
now rheumatoid, anchored aground for years.
You got thrown off after a week, you said –
caught having tea and a fag. Shipped to a tanker,
as your own boss, you skipped off early
on Fridays to smooth-talk girls and dance.

I asked what you'd crafted?
You rubbed your face, buying time,
wiped cheeks veined in seaweed purple
with barnacle knuckles. I offered suggestions:
a mahogany cabinet with dovetails?
An oak bar carved with scrolls, acorns, leaves?

No, you laughed, *the porthole edgings*.
Terms Googled: *King stud* appeared.
I pictured you Elvis-like, easy come easy go.
Your Tony Curtis curl, now white, shook;
you said, you'd trimmed them with *cripples*.

Friday Thirteenth

The silence while we waited after the 999 call. The peace as the paramedic placed a thermometer under your arm, pinched the flesh on the back of your hand, held your wrist. The bitten tongues while we waited to hear if you could answer his questions.

cherry blossom falls
grass littered with confetti
blackbird pecks

The silence as the ECG read the mountains and valleys of your heart. The calmness as we listened to Barry the ambulanceman describe his prized pen, the one he will never use, with the nib crafted from one of NASA's rockets. The dumbness as I worked out what DNR is and my taciturn response, hoping you were unaware as you rested your eyes.

market stalls clear
cars bumper to bumper
single magpie caws

The silence as I joined you in the side-ward, your skin pale saffron in a hospital gown with bright yellow tulips, your white hair limp and stuck to your head. The hush as they hooked you to a drip, I surveyed the view from your City window to plot visible Belfast landmarks. The reticence of my frown when you told me they didn't know where the infection was, even after samples and x-rays. The reserve as I kissed your forehead goodnight.

battleship heavens
downpour rubs out skyline
riverbank bursts

Window Weather

The Icelanders have a word that means just that.
A murky day that you know is better
enjoyed from the comfort of a window-seat;
soft mizzle cleansing leaves shiny and bright.

When webs become crystal dreamcatchers,
or perfect drops form on the telephone lines
and slide slowly down like the oil
on the wire of the indoor rain lamp,

with Venus in pink marble,
her flowing robe revealing perfect curves
against the plastic plants.
Outside the blackbird puffs himself,

feathers rippling. He dances on the lawn.
Drizzle doesn't bring the worms up
but his fancy seven-step has the desired effect
and he pecks and pecks and pecks;

like the drinking woodpecker did, long ago,
on the dentist's counter, see-sawing,
a globe of red liquid dancing, as I looked
past it and through the window,

longing to be outside in the rain.

Cross Roads

When I left school, I crossed a bridge
to work. I was thrown into a world filled
with names I struggled to pronounce.
There I met a boy, from the other side of town.

Friends at first - we talked about our weekends,
shared stories, laughed at youthful antics.
Then I moved, back across the bridge, back
onto familiar roads. We stayed in touch.

Later, we had our own home, mid-terrace,
on a road with coloured kerbs, it didn't matter
which. Inside was neutral, magnolia walls, beige
carpets and a coffee coloured bathroom suite.

City folk, we lived in fear of angry balaclavas;
crossfire cutting communities in two.
Sirens resonated across the Belfast sky.
We took to the roads looking for a haven.

In *The Low Country*, whin bushes shone under
a hay-bale sun, the lough glimmered. Harbour
boats waltzed on golden strands of summer.
Red and black flags adorned main street houses.

A loyal arch, arced across that same road;
we exchanged knowing glances, we wouldn't
be taking chances. Surveyed the site
and soon after foundations were footed.

Years later we migrated; held hands, gold bands,
under a calypso sun and returned as swans.
Added to our brood, just once;
let her choose
which cross to wear,
if any.

Spring Bank Holiday

We travelled far from city noise
to wide skies, woods, wetland
and a lapping lough-shore.
Lego birds had been the bribe.

Leaving Minecraft in the boot
we time-travelled, from plastic blocks
to the kiln, where men had fired
clay bricks. Further back, in the
Crannog's rustic roundhouse,
we stroked hand-daubed clay walls.

Posed for pictures with brick birds
but spent more time feeding the living,
adding new naming words, researching
migration paths, becoming birders.
Pinched your mouth on finding
a yolk-stained shell outside the coop.

Drifting off homeward bound
with shovelers, shelducks, redshanks
flying around your head,
Best day out, EVER, you said.

Until the next one…

Tollymore

Every Easter we worshipped
the steppingstones. Slate
and onyx, bronze, copper
and gold. Little specks
glistened in Spring sunlight.

Cold tickled our flicking
feet. The Shimna giggled
and gurgled, clouds westered,
hugging the Mournes. Hop
skip and jump across and back,

while the tartan rug was
wafted in the wind, cleansed, laid
on daisy and dandelion meadow.
Tupperware offerings arranged,
alongside a flask of tea and Pyrex beakers.

Nanny decided to join in,
got halfway across the stupple,
then slipped. Her hair matted, dripping
blouse transparent, Playtex pointing;
stockings hanging from a limb, to dry,
as her pride swam downriver with the smicks.

Dreamchild

These Strangford wetlands and fields,
inlets, islets and islands,
one for each day of the year,
are your haven; curlew's perfect landscape
of mottled wheat and barley
camouflage, speckled pointed eggs.

Quaver call carried on the breeze
floats through open sash
as I drift off to dreamland.
Ash thin, plane-grey legs
vapour-trailing a cloudless sky
over a moonlit low-tide lough,

transforming into my daughter.
Feathers curl into auburn hair,
down-curved beak becomes a bow
poised to shoot fox mid-flight.
Quiver strapped breast.
She soars towards Scrabo Tower.

Dreamchild returns to lough shore,
Wades at water's edge, where
along Monaghan bank, I'm walking
with a thatched batch of uni stats.
She does not speak, rooting under rocks
shyly searching for shellfish.

Six curlews arrive to join her.
She shrinks, cane legs and crescent
beak reform, feathers return
as she outstretches both wings.
Seven whistlers take flight.
Please – please come home.

Princess of Eiderdown

for my Nieces

In your first Winter,
I guide you into a king-size
ocean; you ride the crest
of the wave, along its middle,
waft a white muslin sail,
laughing at the breeze.
Smiling in a yellow dress,
golden hair radiant,
you are the sun
on my horizon.

Just as I think you are going
to pronounce yourself
Princess of Eiderdown,
in your babbled tongue,
you discover my hand.
Our eyes connect briefly,
and although we have
different bloodlines, I know
we are bound together,
until the vanishing point.

You reach over, clutch
my finger in your tiny
hand, squeeze tight,
strengthen our connection.
Then with the nail,
of your pointing finger,
you pensively pick
at the white moon, rising
from my cuticle;
exploring life's mysteries.

Spiderman

for Vinnie, my Godson

Stuck, limpet strong,
on the glass like a starfish.
Arms outstretched towards space,
curtain-pole-combat-stick ready,
tiptoeing the sill – now a beach
of wall plugs and plaster.

Spiderman impersonation,
scaling the wall,
swinging across the room
on curtained webs
had not played out as planned
and your tears gave the game away.

Sidekick Mum spun you a ladder.
Floored, but resilient, you'll rewrite
the script, play rock songs and dance.
Tonight, you will dream
of ships, stars, outer space;
use my compass to find your way home.

Little Novice

for Fraya

Bowl, wooden spoon, scales
arranged on the bench
like sacraments on the altar.

Flour, butter, eggs;
the holy trinity of sponge.
Little novice at my side;

nervous, excited, chatting
about her white dress, veil,
what the cards could contain.

Flour dusts the worktop
as she teases it from the bag
to the bowl. Just half a spoon more.

Clouds rise on transfer. Into another
she measures silver sugar, golden butter.
Checks her curls in the oven mirror.

She's a tight spring that unwinds
with every revolution of the whisk. I crack
eggs and she beats again, eyes gleaming.

Spatula in hand, she gently folds in flour,
figures of eight, like I've taught her before.
We pray to Honoré the Patron Saint

of baking cakes; frightened for the air
that we don't want to scare.
Buns need bubbles to rise.

Biologist

for Tara

At two, you fell in love. By three,
before fully formed sentences
were within your grasp,
several species circled your tongue.
Knowing their ferocity, geography, anatomy
(first & second dorsal, pectoral, and caudal fin).

Great whites, most dangerous
but you told us it was man's fault
for dressing up as seals.
Followed by tiger, mako, thresher, hammerhead.
Learnt your colours: blue, blacktip, whitetip, gray, and lemon.

Liked the ugly ones best: goblin, wobbegongs.
cried, when you found out honeycomb
and angels were endangered,
decided to be a marine biologist,
an activist, a saviour of sharks.

At eight, you explored *The Blue Planet*.
Posed under a magnificent megalodon jaw
twice your height, its teeth
larger than your fierce hands.
Pressed nose to tank, watched divers with envy.

At nine, you travelled west,
donned a lab coat, rummaged rock pools
and scoured Salthill strand
along the Grattan to Daleysfort Road.
Returned to the lab triumphant

with a sea hare and mermaid's
purse in a clear beaker. You asked them
to safeguard the squishy sea hare,
put the mermaid in maternity;
said goodbye to happy-faced rays.

And now your bookcases
are still-life lined with dusty relics –
ammonites, shells, stones and sharks'
teeth in glass bell-jars;
carpet as dark as the ocean floor.

You study people, bodies, all the *ologies*;
your aspirations metamorphosing,
delving into post-mortem Pathology.
Conversing with death, reaping
its answers is your new cause.

Section 3

A Life Drawn

A Life Drawn

After the exhibition: Leonardo Da Vinci: A Life in Drawing

The cold numbs me. Unlit fire, a deliberate action?
Do my veins protrude more? I am as naked
as a Greek statue and he is in tunic, robes,
headscarves. It makes staying still even harder.

You rarely see a mountain fox stationary
on snow-capped peaks. I want to course
like a hare cross a meadow but I am silent,
sculpture still; running will not feed my family.

He is ferocious with the quill, the goose
feather tip in straight-line motion
as he hatches veracious shadows
on my chest, omits nipple and hair.

Oh! The relief as he asks me to move,
to turn to face the window, bend my arm,
flex the muscles. What is within my grasp?
Temptation to steal, run the risk

of hard labour or the light of a better day,
a steady job with regular pay? He is beside
me now, his breath on what he calls
my scapula. He comes close, to touch

my skin, traces the tendon on my wrist,
follows the eggshell blue line up my arm,
slow journey to shoulder, across neck-bone.
Our eyes do not meet. He inhales me.

Returns to his sketch to add physicality
to lines, curves, light and dark, dimension.
I could converse but he talks to himself,
fast and low, most of the time I do

not understand. He reaches for a knife.
I fear my skin may be too opaque.

American Gothic

After the 1930 painting by Grant Wood

She wore her grandmother's cameo, the only heirloom. Straw-coloured hair, tied back, framing her forlorn face, gaze slant, looking towards a distant town. A careless wisp, willows down the side of her long neck. Not portrayed, is that he inherited his mother's forked tongue and had given her a lashing for this simple sin.

Porch pots of mother-in-law's tongue speak of the great mid-west, monogamy, the American dream. Straight and narrow like weatherboard, the crisp white pin-tuck of his shirt, corrugated barn, puckered lines of the couple's lips, pristine prongs of a pitchfork, and his direct glare.

Five weeks later, the mailman, leaving a parcel on the porch, finds the mister, flat on his back, pitchfork prongs piercing the bib of his dungarees, penetrating his chest cavity between the ribs. His open eyes: matt raw umber. In open jaws, flies shuttle between ochre teeth. White cladding now a splatter-painting, in deep cadmium.

A Lifetime Later

You went up-mountain (the first trip together,
since her belly stopped swelling) to cows
munching lush grass, alpine sun sweetening
milk, scarce supplies for eight children.
Left singing along to cowbells and valley echoes.

For seventy-five years the Tsanfleuron glacier
slithered through the Bernese Alps,
slowly gorging the landscape;
before spitting you out, black and petrified,
clothes and war-time identity papers preserved.

Your watch stopped, our lives froze, when
the crevasse swallowed you. Then you,
weathered, became leathered like the raftered
hides you'd tanned, moulded, stitched;
spellbound into boots.

I wish family ties had been knotted,
tied tight. Instead, our string of paper dolls
was snipped apart and scattered
like snowflakes through the valley.
Strangers, as silent as snowfall.

A lifetime later, the knock.
Knots of not-knowing thaw
like the trickle stream of melting ice.
My cheeks feel snowflakes dissolve,
taking years, the unknown, with them.

Herd

How hard they were to herd, heaving beasts roaming loose,
casually chewing cud and looking at us like mad things.
Delighting in the deliciousness of weed-free grass,
thickened by morning dew and lengthened by a good spell.
Branded with a stubborn streak, they gathered in a gang
and all our *shoo shoo shoo*ing
and *be away with ya now*ing
did nothing to make them reconsider.
They feasted, trampled, turned lawn to sods.

There is a network in villages like this; under the radar
communications, bouncing your troubles between walls
like white noise. Help arrived before we'd asked for it.
Charlie T on a quad, throttling up the driveway,
braking hard, kicking out a gravel cloud. Behind,
wee Tommy T carried willow twice his height.
They dismounted, approached the cattle, surefooted,
sending silent signals, tenderly tapping on flank or rump.

The cows responded filtering into a line,
sauntering in pairs down the drive, through pillars,
up the lane and it was all done without a word.
Swooped shovels, scooped and hurled the still-wet pats,
like sliotars, into the trailer. Shook mute apologies,
then were gone, leaving our dumbfounded laughter
breaking the silence, against the rape-field backdrop
of their invasion, looking at the trodden, sodden lawn.

I Am Not Prepared

I.

I am caught
forever cruciform
against the blue
suspended
Clothed in virgin white
swimming cap borrowed
three paces taken
end of pier a vacuum
I did not freeze
stepped off
legs together
toes *en pointe*
arms outstretched
winged in flight.
Shutter snap.

II.

I see the horizon
fly upwards
close my eyes
pinch my nose
I am not prepared
for the salty sting
of freezing water
crushing my lungs.

III.

My downward rush stops
suspended again
floating in murky bubbles
skirt balloons
I am jellyfish
tentacle legs –
I am not prepared
to break the surface.

Reportage

I denounce him
his intention
to assault
my Mona Lisa smile

Peculiar craving
of human appetite
his power cannot be disputed

the goal
the trolls
the toll

the sun
the mail
the mirror
the times

Centuries of newspaper
incantations
black and white and red

centre spreads

legs spread
she was she did
profit from my sorrow

the destruction
of me
me too
me too

Crucifix hangs from courtroom wall
a reminding force of
male attention

the occult of man's intent
the domination
he exhibits my curves and more

Can I outrun
this race
the ties
the belt

I read your face
I say my name

Lemniscate

In this life, I will walk barefoot
to the holy Ganges and bathe

in polluted waters. Make
sacrifices to end the cycle.

Infinity bows my breasts;
I tie them up, bind them tight, flat.

I conceal my sex and the years,
the rebirths – always a girl

living with simple putdowns
and the terror of toileting at dusk.

Little Magician

His grubby pointing finger
reaching towards the buckle
would make me play statue.

'Do you want me to take it off?'
'Do you want to feel the belt?'
Threats, serious and often.

The game changed – Polly put the kettle on –
'In a minute Daddy, I'm colouring in'.
A lion tamer whipped the belt at my feet.

Game changed again – musical chairs –
I'd stand on his shoulders, touching
the ceiling, arms outstretched, flying high.

My legs slid down his chest,
I hugged his head, pleased
with my amazing balancing act.

He lifted me over his head, twirled me
round mid-air, brought me slowly to the floor,
told me what a good girl I could be.

Played Nurse Nancy next. Him in bed
hungover. A heap of crumpled
clothes at the foot of the divan

looking like a snake charmer's basket.
I grabbed the forked tongue and ran.
Coiled it up, shoved it behind…

Waved an arm.
Abracadabra – vamoose!
                        Never to be found.

Handwritten

Words inked in white,
invisible to your glare.
Or spun in gossamer
strands within spiders' webs
in ceiling corners because
you never look up.

Your eyes focus downwards;
your stare always slant.
Your words: stinging offensives,
smarting objections. Imprinted
on skin in yellow and purple;
I plant irises for Spring.

Demolition

In black and white;
back arched
eyes down
he strongman poses
at the weakest point
of the bridge.

Tip-toes on keystone
like a marble god
in combats
biceps bulging
conjuring destruction.

Sledgehammer set
to thrust it out
send it crumbling
into deep darkness.

The Starry Night

I inherited this property from the preacher;
pure biblical relations. My windows
offer nothing of Vincent's cosy glow.
Outside these stone walls
there's a vast pasture, a vacuum.

My sky is a straight Van Gogh void of Indian yellow,
swirl-less. White slits of shooting stars slash
ultra-marine and cobalt blue Kansas canvas.

Planet-less – no Venus or crescent Moon
just a million pinprick stars
above a washed-out wheat-field.

Termite towers of tea chests,
stalagmites of soap (cleanliness is next
to godliness), columns of catalogues
and pillars of papers
come in and never leave.

My door is locked,
three times.
Religiously.

The World's Most Dangerous Harpist

for Ursula Burns

She is Erin personified. Her dress
always grass green; long velour gown
hugging voluptuous curves, with a slit
up to her hip and plunging neckline
revealing rounds of plump flesh.

I suspect there may be a zigzag welt beneath
those breasts, the scar of an Imperial lion
that tried to pull her apart, when harps were
burned and harpists hounded, hung, hunted
to near extinction. She is a survivor and yet

for many years she was caged, confined to culture,
grew long nails to pluck. Taken to entertain, set out
in front of the gentry to be gawked at. Even now
she still loses her head, plays traditional concertos
instead of satiric comedy in a key the opposite of F.

Her harp is cut from a single piece of willow.
Carved by skilful faeries, intricate unending
patterns; cornucopia crown of foliage and flowers.
Strings bestowed by Scottish Unicorns; as soft as silk
with dragon's strength, they shine in the darkness.

Her hair, colours of Autumn blaze, linen flax
at nightfall, bronze brooches; waterfalls over shoulders,
down her back, flows in meandering rivulets
to her waist. She used to conceal its rarity
under dull brown or barely black - not now.

Now, she stands on stage in a blood red room
acting the fool. But she's no clown - don't y'know
she's the world's most dangerous harpist?
For the finale she lies down, rolls and writhes,
thrums the quavering harp between bent knees,

to bring us all to a climax.

The Vampire of Lazzaretto Vecchio

Reflection of a reverential sunrise
on calm waters; sailing to the sanatorium
in the white boat. White for the uncontaminated
the blessed and clean.

I don the doctor's mask, pomander of herbs, lavender
and roses – so sweet. Add boots, long leather gown, hat;
armour against bites from fleas, rats and the mad men,
who at the end, run wild into the gardens
to crucify themselves on thorns.

As the sun arcs across the sky, the stench rises too
I make rounds, observations, try treatments.
Rancid heat retreats at dusk, the sick wards weep
like religious statues, infecting the air with howls for help.

Plagued with death, five hundred a day,
the grounds become a necropolis
where mass grave is layered
on mass grave;
strata of decay.

A Monatto crouches on the mound,
agitated and thrashing. I see the soil
is scraped back, as if by the claws of a ravenous monster,
revealing the recently deceased;
one body, his only concern.

Fists, fingerless and black, breaking through
earth either side of her head.
Open mouth gaping; no longer secret
secretions; boils bursting.

Now it's clear what his panic is.
A shroud-eater on the island.
The living dead will consume us all.

I lift a brick, ram it in her mouth,
hear teeth fracture like alabaster,
or a resurrected creature, crumbling.
Look at the blasphemous sunset.

At Castle Ward

After a photograph displayed in Down County Museum, Downpatrick.

The photographer was well-used to the rich and famous, their poses carefully thought out and props well chosen to reflect status, virtue, valour. Those commonly carried included: doubled-barrel shotguns, crisp linen hankies, walking sticks and The Bible. Today, both men are in their best three-piece suits. The Viscount dressed darkly, black top hat and tie, formal wool suit (double-breasted), white winged-collar shirt, as pointed as his white moustache and beard. Sitting on a wrought iron bench, left arm extended along the top bar, showing his width, breadth, reach. The Admiral is in tweed, a well-placed pocket handkerchief and loosely looped bowtie, standing behind the seat. Until now, the photographer thinks things are perfectly normal 'til the groundsman places a British Bulldog on the bench. His name, the dog that is, is Plato and he is dressed in Sunday best. Shirt, cravat, coat, tweed flat-peaked cap. His front paw placed on the curved handle of a blackthorn walking stick. The cameraman must capture this quickly, before Plato runs across the gardens of Castle Ward on the scent of last night's fox.

picture an admiral, a viscount
an old soul in a young dog's face
Plato the philosopher.

Scrabo Cheirotherium Fossil

Empty metal claws
mounted in Down museum
missing your footprint.

The Day the Painting Came Alive

After 'The Green Coat' by Sir John Lavery (1856-1941) and a living history event at the Ulster Museum, Belfast.

Having missed the moment, she was already
present, on the solid floor when we arrived,
stepped out from the painting's heavy frame.

Replicating her picture pose,
rearranging the viridian green silk coat
(not really a coat – more shawl with fringed trim).

Had she sensed her painted world
begin to soften? Threshold blur,
heard the mantle clock's rhythmic tick,
smelt beeswax furniture polish,
felt padded Axminster underfoot,
watched dancing dust motes
in sunlight, coming through
the window on her right?

We welcomed her, called her Hazel
with this century's informality.
The gracious lady posed for *selfies*,
I'm sure she wondered what magic
made instant pictures.
Then Sir John approached, three dimensional,
with dark moustache, foreboding eyes,
and we could not gauge her expression
as she looked right through him.

Still life with hedgehog

The items have been arranged;
carefully positioned, to vary height
with texture and tone. Lit from the left.

But what the artist hadn't bargained for
was that the sleeping urchin would unfurl;
spine straightening, light-tipped quills oblique,

to nimbly negotiate the spray of red roses,
and feast on wedge of watermelon.
White table linen turning light pink.

Notes and Glossary

The Lock
- O'Neill's Red Hand – also known as the red hand of Ulster. There is an Irish legend that states that during a boat race of chieftains O'Neill cut off his hand because the first to touch the shore would be King of Ireland.
- Arrol gantries – the large steel frameworks, including travelling cranes and lifts, around the slipways where the ships were being constructed. Designed and built by Sir William Arrol & Co. for Harland & Wolff
- Dunchers – the name given to the flat cap hats worn by the labourers. Foremen wore bowler hats.

The Port of the Bog
- Portavogie comes from the Irish Port a' Bhogaigh meaning Harbour of the Bog and is a fishing village on the North-east coast of Ireland. Years ago, my uncle, a local fisherman burnt his trawler in protest against EU fishing quotas.

Dead Short on the System
- The curfew – Ireland was going through a period of civil war. A curfew was brought in to curb riotous violence.

Annadale, 22nd April 1914
- The women's suffrage movement in Ireland were ramping up their campaign and some resorted to breaking the law. One such event occurred at Annadale Hall, a mansion house in South Belfast which was set on fire. The house was vacant but had had many notable inhabitants, namely members of the Massereene family of Antrim Castle, the Duke of Wellington's Mother, a Colonal and a Justice of the Peace.

Domestic Help, 1916
- Cumann na mBan – The league of women, formed in Dublin in 1914, to complement the republican Irish Volunteer Force.
- Céilí – an Irish dance with folk music
- Mauser – a type of German rifle used in the uprising
- Six days – the length of the Easter Rising
- Say I do – Joseph Plunkett married his fiance, Grace Gifford, at Kilmainham Gaol eight hours before his execution.
- Don't wear black – Grace wore her widow's mourning clothes for the rest of her life.

Christmas Morning, Carrowdore, 1870
- Inspired by the cover image of Sons of the Sod by W.G. Lyttle
- Tummock – Ulster Scots for a low-lying paddock.

Wully Yeaman at the Punch Ball
- Temper's aizy riz – Ulster Scots for easily angered
- The Punch Ball – an annual dance in Carrowdore

Benin to Belfast
- Benin – the Kingdom of Benin is now modern-day Nigeria
- Oba – the ruler of the Edo people of Benin
- Crafters Guild – in Benin City, craft workers were organised into groups called guilds. The only group allowed to work for the Oba was the most important one, the brass caster's guild
- Admiral Rawson – In 1897 the British force, under the command of Admiral Sir Harry Rawson, exiled the Oba and took control of the area. Known as the Punitive Expedition it ended with Benin being burnt to the ground and the country's treasured artwork and Benin Bronzes being stolen.
- Civil Rights Movement – The Northern Ireland Civil Rights Movement, inspired by the ongoing campaign for civil rights in the US, challenged inequality and discrimination in Northern Ireland. Protests took place during the late 1960s at the same time as 'The Troubles' were starting.

Only Footprints
- Eugene Cernan – known as Gene, he was an American astronaut and the last person to walk on the moon.

Belfast Moon
- The renewable heat incentive (RHI) scheme scandal, which became know as the Cash For Ash scandal, was a political scandal in Northern Ireland which led to the collapse of the Northern Ireland Executive at Stormont.

Duck, duck, goose
- Poem inspired by an article in a local newspaper – 2017 https://www.belfasttelegraph.couk/news/environment/geese-under-loyalist-paramilitaries-wing-make-belfast-shankill-estate-home-35439757.html
- Duck, duck, goose – is a traditional children's game.
- Shankill Estate – a Loyalist housing estate in Belfast

Home
- Ulster Worker's Council Strike – a strike which took place, during The troubles, in May of 1974. It was overseen by the Ulster Worker's Council and the Ulster Army Council. Both groups had members of the UDA and UVF. These strikes were held to protest against the Sunningdale Agreement and a power-sharing local parliament.
- UDA – Ulster Defence Association
- UVF – Ulster Volunteer Force

Foot Reading
- Mournes – The Mountains of Mourne are a range of granite mountains in County Down.
- Skim for smicks – catching little fish, like sticklebacks, in a handheld net
- Shimna – a river which flows from the Ott Mountain, in the Mourne Mountains to the coastal village of Newcastle and into the sea in Dundrum Bay.

Faith
- Whip and peerie – a childs toy consisting of a spinning top (the peerie) and a stick with a length of string (the whip)

Coupes
- The Floral Hall – was built in the 1930s for the Belfast Corporation (which later became Belfast City Council) as part of the Bellevue Zoo leisure complex and is located in the north of the city. It was a very popular dance hall.
- Fifty yards of net – my mother made her own clothing, including her ball gowns. The pink one in this poem had a huge skirt made with 50 yards of net and sequins hand stitched.

Bridging
- The Albert – a bridge in Belfast which crosses the river Lagan, it is well-known for the murmerations of starlings in the evenings

Job No. 1621
- King stud and cripples – are both carpentry terms for the timber supports either side of a window.

Window Weather
- The Icelandic word meaning window weather is Gluggaveður
- Drinking bird – toy heat engines, in the late seventies my dentist had one that looked like a woodpecker. For the scientific explanation I recommend an internet search.

Cross Roads
- The Low Country – the local name for the part of the lower Ards Peninsula. The Ards Peninsula is a hurling stronghold within County Down.
- Red and black flags – red and black is the colour of the County Down hurling team kit. Supporters decorate their cars and houses with flags on match day to show their support. Hurling is predominately played by Catholics
- Loyal arch – The Loyal Orange Institution, commonly know as the Orange Order, is a Protestant organisation. Sometimes they will erect decorative arches across the road, near or outside Orange Lodge buildings.

Tollymore
- Stupple – steppingstones
- Smicks – colloquial name for small fish like sticklebacks

Dreamchild
- I wrote this poem for an anthology on endangered birds being published by the Beautiful Dragons. I was given the Curlew to write about. Whilst researching curlews I discovered that in mythology they often signify parental loss. As my daughter was looking at potential universities I imagined this dream sequence.
- Strangford Lough – is the largest inlet in the British Isles. It is in the East of Northern Ireland and is almost totally enclosed by the Ards Peninsula but is linked to the Irish Sea by a long narrow channel.

A Lifetime Later
- Poem inspired by newspaper article – 2017 https://www.nbcnewscom/news/world/swiss-couple-missing-75-years-found-melting-alps-glacier-n784311

Herd
- Sliotar – a hard leather-covered ball used in the game of hurling. Hurling is one of the most ancient Irish outdoor team games.

Lemniscate
- Lemniscate – the name for the sign of infinity ∞

The Vampire of Lazzaretto Vecchio
- This poem was inspired by a visit to the Forensic Anthropology Department, at John Moore University in Liverpool, during which I heard Dr Borrini recount the story of finding a skeleton with a brick in its mouth on an Italian plaque island. You can read more here: https://www.livescience.com/3374-medieval-vampire-skull.html

Acknowledgments

Thanks are due to the following publications in which some of the poems, or versions of them, were first published: *A New Ulster, Atrium, The Bangor Literary Journal, Boyne Berries, The Bramley (*Volumes 1 and 2*), The Cabinet of Heed*, Community Arts Partnership Anthologies *Matter, Resonance and Vision, FourXFour, Her Other Language: Northern Irish Women Address Domestic Violence and Abuse* (Arlen House, 2020)*, The Honest Ulsterman, If You Believe They Put A Man on the Moon* (Hedgehog Poetry Press, 2019)*, The Interpreter's House, Light: A Journal of Poetry and Photography, The Blue Nib, The North, Ode to a Hedgehog (*Hedgehog Poetry Press, 2018*), The Peeking Cat Anthology* (2017)*, The Road to Clevedon Pier* (Hedgehog Poetry Press, 2018)*, Songs to Learn and Sing* (Hedgehog Poetry Press, 2018)*, Visual Verse* and *Watch the Birdie* (Beautiful Dragons, 2018).

From Benin to Belfast was longlisted in the Pendle War Poetry Competition, 2018. *Reportage* (previously titled *Odin's Court*) was highly commended in the Lenin and McCarthy Competition from Hedgehog Poetry Press, 2019. *Job No. 1621* won the July (2019) Creative Writing Ink monthly competition. *Fire-Lighting* won the 7th Annual Bangor Poetry Competition. *Duck, duck, goose* was longlisted for the 2020 Seamus Heaney Award for New Writing. *Little Magician* received a notable mention in the Cúirt New Writing Prize for Poetry, 2020

This is now my third publication with Hedgehog Poetry Press and I am, and always will be, indebted to Mark Davidson for the unwavering belief he has in me as a poet. His sense of humour, kindness and patience all make the editorial process a joy.

I would like to thank the Arts Council of Northern Ireland (ACNI) for their generosity in awarding funding through the Support for the Individual Artist Programme which allowed me to develop professionally. Some poems were written and edited in The River Mill and I offer my gratitude to Paul Maddern for his hospitality, particularly the lemon tart. The award also allowed me the privilege of being mentored by, the very talented poet, Maria McManus and I'm grateful for her guidance and encouragement. Thanks also to Damian Smyth, Head of Literature and Drama at ACNI, for his advice and support.

I hope you like the book cover as much as I do. It is the wonderful work of David Goring at 2789 Graphic Design, all I did was tell him the title. I love it, thanks Dave!

Huge thanks to Holywood Writer's Group for their friendship, feedback and encouragement. Much appreciation to those who have written blurbs and taken the time to do close readings, specifically: Eileen Carney Hulme, Heather Lowry, Karen Mooney, Maria McManus and Trish Bennett. I would like to acknowledge the local writing community (of which there are too many to name individually) for opportunities and support but they will know who they are.

Lastly, but most importantly, I would like to recognise the support of my friends and family. They have been there to celebrate successes, to support me during rejections, periods of writer's block, feelings of self-doubt and imposter syndrome and I appreciate that more than words can say. My husband Michael has great patience, which is probably why we are still together. He has had to put up with many a meltdown by me, as I put this collection together. He is also a great proof-reader but if you have spotted an error that is somebody else's fault. Thanks for putting up with me, Michael! My daughter, Tara, is my harshest critic, she keeps me grounded and is great at making the launch buns. Thank you, Tara! Thanks to my parents, Tony and Valerie Carson, for being so hardworking and setting a great example as I was growing up. I'm lucky to have a great set of in-laws, Roy, Jean and the rest of the Kane clan. I am really sad that Jean didn't get to see this book. She is sorely missed. Along with my extended family and ancestors, they have all been a great source of inspiration for many of the poems in this book. Without them this book would not have happened. Without readers there would be no point, so much appreciation to all you readers! Thank you so much.

"Kane's poems are Ulster poems; authentic, lived, and as intimate as Super 8 films. Close reading gives us glimpses of the domestic and the near-past, reel on reel, frame by frame. As readers we are inside the poems, part of a narrative distinctly of place, of community, and of the familial. Days out, work, ancestry, landscape; these things are peopled with the weight of history and happenstance. The context she exposes is affectionate, but it is always also navigating rules, code and the complexities of a place and people riven with its distinct, hardwired contradictions; the past and the contemporary, cheek by jowl."

>Maria McManus, author of *Available Light* (Arlen House), *We are Bone* (Lagan Press), *The Cello Suites* (Lagan Press) and *Reading the Dog* (Lagan Press).

"In Venus in pink marble, Kane takes the reader on an honest journey through her own personal history and experiences. It is at once powerful and far reaching, unafraid to tackle big political themes or to offer a tender and loving exploration of family and relationships. The final section includes bold and imaginative perspectives on artwork moving the poems from inward to outward."

>Eileen Carney Hulme, author of *Stroking the Air* (Bluechrome), *The Space Between Rain* (Indigo Dreams) and *The Stone Messenger* (Indigo Dreams).

Gaynor Kane fell into writing accidentally. At forty, instead of buying a mid-life crisis sports car, she started a degree with the Open University. She finished her BA (Hons) in Humanities with Literature in 2016, with a module on creative writing. Since then, she has been widely published and has been placed in several poetry competitions. Now, at fifty, she is happy to be publishing her full collection, *Venus in pink marble*. It was always her aspiration that this collection would come into the world in 2020, she just didn't think it would be amid a global pandemic. Gaynor has two other publications with The Hedgehog Poetry Press, they are *Circling the Sun* (2018) and *Memory Forest* (2019). You can read more about them at www.gaynorkane.com.

Follow Gaynor at Facebook: @gaynorkanepoet

                on Twitter: @gaynorkane

Lightning Source UK Ltd.
Milton Keynes UK
UKHW040637011120
372596UK00001B/48